CULTURATION

The Unrelenting Contemporization
of Modern Identity and the
Failure of Individual
Authenticity

J. D. Stewart

Cover images purchased from iStock.com and modified for
the design of this cover.

ISBN 9781516955824

Natural man is entirely for himself. He is numerical unity, the absolute whole which is relative only to itself or its kind. Civil man is only a fractional unity dependent on the denominator; his value is determined by his relation to the whole, which is the social body.

Emile, Jean-Jacques Rousseau

TABLE OF CONTENTS

Introduction

Whether natural or civil man we are all the victims of culture, society and culturation. We may all have incomplete identities, inauthentic even borrowed personas. We have not been captured but have willingly and often been cultured by the involuntary contemporization of our lives. Culturation is used here to refer to the process by which humans live in a world for which the changes wrought in their lives are not completely voluntarily constructed the implications of our surrender are not always understood. We are both enculturated from birth and face the effects of innovation and acculturated in conflicting cultural understandings throughout our lives. Enculturation is a process by which people are moved from their attitudes and dispositions to the inadvertently accepted flow of the cultural ship beginning from birth and parental influences. Acculturation is the battle between cultural forces for indwelling support and is a battle met from all side in which ones understanding of self, others and the world around chips away at enculturated tenets.

Increasingly, however, involuntary cultivation challenges our beliefs since we are incapable of responding, testing and certifying all the changes to which we are exposed on a daily basis. The application of the root word "culture" has taken a long run to end up with a scientific, more to the point, often bacteriological usage. When bacteria or fungi or some other microorganisms are "cultured," it means that they are grown on a media or nutritive substance, often in a petri dish. The microorganisms are spread out, in the inoculating sample, and those bacteria that can use the nutrition provided will grow involuntarily and will usually be visible in time as macroscopic colonies of homologous and identifiable strains. Color, or colors, even textures of the organisms may make possible the identification of the organisms on the media, each individual bacterial cell identical to others in its colony or contributing to the cultural identity.

Their growth is a function of the effect of their environment. To be grown as lower forms in a culture tube and only manifest that which is dictated by the influence of our surroundings is this our fate? We are, like microorganism, "cultured" such that as groups, communities, corporations or merely individuals we are grown passively on the restrictive diet of rapid modern change, possibly grown or cultured in megalithic high-rise structures to the veritable cloning of life styles and loci, or within a cultural grouping where individuals share and become the invariable reflection of other group members.

Modernity provides its own assumptions that, for some people, certifies vitality, while others may wither. Most of us grow under the influence of the surrounding culture, and, if not healthy and changed for the better, we are maintained contemporaneously with the resultant changes that the culture imbues being unrecognized and, therefore, not judged for suitability or analyzed for contributing value to our lives. In rapid succession change reanimates us giving us new descriptive identity. With time we relinquish ourselves to what may seem only technology or social imperatives which change the way we act and think.

We may jump all in as we are regrown from sustenance, from unrecognized sources, trusting its quiet infiltration into our meta-compositional psyches to be positive. The cumulative effects are almost never noticed, inculcated through gradualism by which we believe that these changes occurs. The network of change, however, is unrelenting, growing around and in us everyday.

We could view the change in our world by cataloging everything that happens, say, over a year's time. All material changes as well as any attitudinal change could be documented and comparisons made. It would be relatively easy, if not time consuming, to find the physical differences in the annual comparisons, but the unseen, attitudinal changes, may not be so easily detected, since we may eliminate from our survey factors we think are not important such as clothes, cars, houses and friends, while other factors we may believe are obliviously influencing us. Some factors may be thought of as merely personal considerations, and it may be believed that they hold no transformative powers. Such items as cell phones and TVs maybe seen as not influential at all but may be thought of as merely providing accessibility to information, neutral in our self-definition.

Objects that find their way into our daily lives may alter our temperament. When Cell phones have been commandeered and the owners made unable to call or answer a ringing phone, they may show extreme anxiety. We can tell ourselves that it is just a phone but out attitude does not reinforce our admission of the phone being merely a device of convenience. The phone under these circumstances, has become a needed object of self-definition in our lives. Many would choose to text using their phones rather than actually meeting others in person for personable face-to-face interactions. This impersonal meeting has become so prevalent that authentic interaction among friends and colleagues is often seen as relatively unimportant.

Computers, televisions and cars are objects of modern life that interfere with genuine social involvement and change our lives in ways that we may not notice or understand. This book hopes to chronicle these influences and others in our lives pointing up our overpowering and stark passivity by which we have become deaf and blind to the factors that take us off course one effect at a time and over time. The measure of today's expectations are due in large part to societies cultivation of our lives, molded in form and pattern to that of those around us such that we may become unrecognizable to those in our surroundings, and, far greater in effect, the loss of ourselves to the cloning which precludes our finding our own unique identity.

Chapter 1

The New World

The ancients reinforced group identity from generation to generation. It was conserved as it was passed along. Those that broke ranks and displayed alternate character were seen not as valuable individuals but rather as those that were defiant, rejecting authority. Family induced conformity, enculturation, often resulted in pressing the young into family business and arranged marriages which tended to maintained the family traditions, money and business. In colonial times children were often little more than indentured servants because of adherences to family directives from their youth. There was hardly a potential for finding a way for oneself when controlled in life by familial circumstance from the cradle to the grave.

But we are living in the modern age where to be different and rebellious is considered being an individual. We have been possessed by the idea, at least since the Enlightenment Project, that we have been set free from others. As described in Aldous Huxley's *Brave New World*, a book about a far reaching view of what was to come and how the individual stood in the midst of a labelling and dis-individualizing culture, we seem, as described in the book, to be living this brave new world today in many ways. Like the ancients we are being hewn by the culture to be what it has willed for us and we have only just begun our perpetual journey as social decerebrates in trans-culturation. Socrates was forced, or rather he chose, to drink the poison which killed him because he diverged to far from the *status quo* but would not repent. This drastic step for principle would not draw us to finalize a revolt against the opposing influences around us. We do not protest but protect ourselves and easily succumb to environmental influences.

What is coming into our future consists of physical and psychological changes, a veritable radically new world and we are just beginning to see the trends. These changes are difficult to imagine. As Yogi Bara amusingly commented: the future is not what it used to be. These changes that would bring us into a world of electronic relationships and placid following of often nebulous influences, more widespread than we see now, where relationships are formed and broken without ever actually having the opportunity of seeing each other in the flesh or acquiescing to the *zeitgeist* without necessarily paying respect to the ever pressing yet gentle allegiance acquired to the enveloping forces that work around us.

Our domestic and work lives may be so much different because of this new dynamic. It may be that an employer may hire, fire and retire workers in the future without ever seeing them. As international companies become truly international in the sense that employees that are needed for the work are dispersed over the face of the earth and since job qualifications may be extremely specialized, and only the rare employee will be able to do the work, the workforce may be decentralized. Employees may work for multiple companies and even be employed by phantom corporations which will exist without a solitary physical location. Workers may live and spend most if not all of their lives in a high rise or a high-rise complex. Other employees may not have a set physical locations from which they may travel for the company. They may spend their time in hotels associated with airports all over the world, never having a fixed location, no place to call home.

This could be our brave new world. The trend toward greater hyper-specialization and socialization is beginning to arise everywhere. Even children are being sacrificed at the drop of the bosses hat to a place away from the town or city in which they were born or where they were going to school. Change and relocation will be the rule for most young people and their families in the future, if a domestic work plan includes the option of marriage.

The family is in doubt. For the first time in America intact families with children represent less than fifty percent of all families. Marriages rise and fall in numbers, but there is a good chance that most grandparents might inherit a lifelong commitment to their grandchildren, raising them and serving as parents *in absentia*. Trust has waned as circumstances outside the authority of marriage seem to threaten even newlyweds and long-guarded marriages. It would seem that the cresting waves of change are sweeping young marrieds into unknown waters. Vows intended for all time are being scrapped for new jobs, new job relationships, as a result of both husband and wife working, the usual recipe for the young building a home, has been replaced with social media, in which you become acquainted with people you have never seen only to become closer to them than to one who shares your house and bed. Between the move up in ones job status and the social networking with a potentially unlimited people base, home fires may dim and embers die. One day a married man or woman awakes to a home partner that they do not know, a better friend to a selective world of social friends than to an avowed mate. We have seen the beginning of this transformation of lives, but the future will bring effects that introduce a massive change in these regards and possibly because of changes we might not notice or not understand.

This seems quite serious, and it is. The ideal family since ancient times has depended on the family closeness, face-to face ties to strengthen and embolden nations. In war and famine man has always clung to the family for support. Every thing was passed along to the children, who have been modeled by parents. How to behave, dress and eat was directed and even taught through experience.

But some just never get the lesson. Some are protected from their seduction by the culture, while others are taken in and are blind to influences that make them victim to culturation's broad influence. I was in a deli the other day and a young, grown gentleman had only placed iceberg lettuce in his bowl for despite having paid for the salad bar, he did not recognize any of the other foods available. The possibility of potato salad, pasta salad, artichoke hearts and olives, did not seem to register with him. The buffet items were not disliked by him, they were unknown to him. Certainly in asking me what they were would indicate he had little knowledge of salads or any of the possible ingredients that might be chosen to put a salad together. He may have eaten fast food or one-menu meals at home from the cradle. I felt sorry for him and tried to help him make decisions, but after he had stopped asking me questions about the salad-bar fare, he was still mulling over the possibilities for fifteen minutes. From where I was sitting with my friends, I saw him scrutinizing and agonizing over the salad ingredients for which he had paid without adding more choices to his bowl. Although children may be finicky in their choice of food, adults, in time, have usually learned to appreciate foods and salad, recognizing the ingredients. I wondered if this young man would have that experience.

But this is not primary change that threatens to re-culturate the way we live and possibly who we are, as far as we can see. It is merely the result of pyramidal change that passes its effects down producing myriad complications. An example of such a broad sweeping effect can be seen in rapid technology. What if some new technological development were to change almost everything around you. There is a very good example that threatens just that. Graphene could become a revolutionary new material. It is a carbon material that could change everything from car manufacture to batteries. Lighter than air, strong by many times that of steel it could have endless applications for present technologies and may usher in new technologies never before imagined. Most of the manufacturing materials like plastic, carbon fiber and steel could be replaced. It may be expensive at first but then ubiquity will make it quite affordable. What then will happen to steel production and the plastics industry. Gasoline consumption could drop 80 % or more. Plastics from oil products may become a thing of the past. No need for electric cars since the lightness of the material for cars could decrease gas mileage beyond that of hybrids and current electric cars.

How does this change the stock market, oil and steel prices not to mention the secondary market areas impacted by this new technology. In graphene's move to prominence what massive changes will ultimately change not just what we do, and how we do it but who we are? It is hard to imagine that such radical technology would not drastically change how we live.

In the future we may be radically changed by both impersonal and personal effects. To avoid our incorporation into the merging future vortex, we must analyze and test everything new that comes into our lives.

Chapter 3

Identity

How do we learn who we are. If we do not recognize, let alone eat, well known menu items, we are adrift in a culture where the common place, the food, say, that unites a people is unknown to younger Americans. If so then what are the depths of marginality. Others believe because they like and eat all foods even foods of foreign lands that that makes them cosmopolitan. England which is said in the main to have the most horrendous native food, has developed the taste for Indian food from the days of the Raj. In many common British communities that do not benefit from young internationally trained chefs, Indian could be that the only accessible edible food.

Likewise, world travel does not necessarily broaden our cultural understanding or toleration. Our identity may come from many areas of influence, but our habits in eating and travel often do not help us and possibly may keep us from knowing or expressing who we really are, if we absorb its influences too deeply into acceptance of the other.

Clothes, cars and houses are often a definitive measure of ones level of education or professional success. This assessment may tell more about what you might do for a living but not necessarily who you are. Multicultural influences do not always make us more tolerant as much as possibly more unsure of who we are through our mimicking personal choices and affectations of others.

The major problem from youth is that we tend to become what we do rather than establishing an identity and then developing a working profile from our distinct talents and predispositions. When I retired from teaching in public high school, I believed that I would do something else. I had left the laboratory to teach science, so I just needed to move on to some other interest as I had before, but six months later I was in tears. I did not know who I was. My identity had been given me by my responsibility to teach young people, just as my identity had be given by my prior occupation and both had come to an end. My brother has since died, but a year and a half before I lost him, he helped me with the lack of purpose and the sensory deprivation that I was experiencing. Yet the advice that he left me with was a defensive strategy: If I go out to buy a gallon of milk in the morning, then that would be a good and full day. This was little more than a mantra for not having a full life. This down-grading of life's potential was little more than learning to greet each day with little or no expectations, which may have been good for him but not for me. I loved my brother, but realized that he had few options left, as I was left without great expectations but little in the way of hope for a new and vital employment interest, I was floundering, looking for direction that had always been predetermined by my vocation at the time.

Giving new direction to my life took several difficult years. What I had not worked out was that except for teaching I had been going through unanalyzed change for decades. This was the mark of our age, and I had not recognized it. Over three or four decades, I had become a different person. I had left any identity that I had before teaching, and, now in retirement, I had no independent knowledge of myself to fall back on.

Not because of age but because the world was swirling and turning around me, I had changed with it without reason, without questioning. Nothing in the end would change. I would once again become what I did as I had before and stand amazed at the me that was being made from what I thought was my own doing. I had moved through marathoning, to art classes, to building stained glass windows, to lab work and finally to teaching without realizing that I did what I did within the environmental constraints of a world that captured me easily by mostly unseen and certainly unrecognized influences. My social and political leanings were considerably different and the environment changed my habits, not through thought. I was a function of the rapid and often scary changes in the world around me. I was not actively seeking a new view of the world but was reacting to it.

Who am I? Who are you? Do my actions or yours represent more than the reflexive jerk of a idea or a response that does not quite make its meaning clear. The worst outcome of living life this way is that one never has to come to terms with our actions or thought processes but instead may drift with the *zeitgeist* being conformed to the larger unthought flow of ideas and actions. Terror divides our world; our activities keep us from developing a meaningful understanding of who they are and who we have to become to survive. We become in some sense potential thought terrorists, willing to commit to an unanalyzed effect in our own lives and those around us. How do we understand who they are when we are absorbing an identity for ourselves, and acting on cultural proxy. The young are being won over by social media to terror or supporting terror. Without an understanding of who they are, they are likely to find identity in a fashionable terrorist future. Our country, at that point, will become an unanalyzed and changing culture under whose authority America can not survive.

Chapter 3

Rapid Change

How many phones have you owned in the last ten years? Did you change because your old phone did not work? Or did you feel that you were not contemporary without the latest apps? Recycle shops like Salvation Army, Junior League and Goodwill all depend on people parting with their belongings long before they are no longer useful. Phones, shoes, shirts, slacks, sweaters and more are given away before they are noticeably worn and many are resold. Our justification for making our no longer wanted items is not that we are charitable so much as we wish to be up-to-date.

Computers and accessories are recycled for precious metal content. This has been made a more likely possibility, since new software and software updates are not always compatible with older computers. Scanners, Fax machines and copiers, at some point, do not have the software developer's support for the older hardware encouraging the purchase of new computers and accessories. Apple Classic computer, originary from the early 80s, had its platform overhauled in the early 2000s such that earlier software written for earlier models would no longer work on the newer models. In computer years this long Apple linage that allowed computer owners to carry very old software over to new model computers was virtually unheard of in the PC market. Apple determined the rules for developer hardware and software in its monolithic world, whereas Microsoft had to contend with looser rule for many times the number of developers, for unyielding independence in writing programs. There were many hardware producers of PC units that found co-ordination with PC platforms could be less demanding, thus carrying over software to new units was fraught with incompatibilities among PC computer manufacturers.

Our turnaround time for large ticket items is short. Cars are traded frequently, considering the cost to individual budgets. Driving down the street, you do see some old cars, but it seems that a great majority are new or relatively new. Before this interminable recession, a car was traded less than every 5 years. Today, because of the economic woes, a car is kept between 6 and 7 years and then traded. It seems most of us want new or newer cars, despite that we have taken wiser counsel in the throes of recent economic hard times. For the most part, cars are quite dependable and will give good service for a decade or more, but we want the new, since an older car reflects our not being in touch with life in general — old car, old ideas. We have seen old people so often driving old cars. These elderly citizens are thought to be out of touch with new ideas and innovation, but they may be, for the most part, only unable to replace the old car for the cost of a new or newer car. It may not make sense for a senior to keep updating automobiles, if all the driving that is done is to the grocery store and the doctors' offices. But for those who would be the victims of culturation, new cars or newer used cars may stand for embracing the new without being cognizant of their compliance with the mandate for innovation.

For those who are fashionably innovative, change may be a disease. It impacts our dress, our cars and even our wives and husbands. We drive new cars on woefully tortured city streets which only tears them up but we insist on getting new or newer cars only to have them literally fall apart on us under these road stresses. Our homes have become the cutting edge of electronic surveillance. We are able, in just the last several years, to adjust the house temperature, open or lock the doors to the house, view dogs sleeping in their beds and turn on the oven to cook a roast. As the sun moves across the sky we can protect against elevated temperatures or reduced temperatures by programming our electronic window shades to open and close as needed. Soon we will have driverless cars and will be able to travel to a neighboring city while we play dominoes. There will be no physical area of our life that we cannot control from our phone from anywhere in the world. Do we need these innovations? Have we even thought that there could be a down side to such rapid change

Although these innovations have been possible for many years. It only required a company to make them simple to use and changeable from a phone at our fingertips to make this a desirable option in our lives. Once it became economically feasibly and easily set up even the home security systems began to incorporate them in their bundled services. Why do we do these tweaks to our lives? We do not want to be seen by our neighbors as Luddites. Apart from hatred of progress the only other explanation must be stupidity. I met a man who had been on the ground floor of the Bill Gates computer phenomenon, who, two decades ago, had cameras all around his desert mansion in Arizona so when he was away he could monitor it. Because of the seclusion of his home, it seemed more likely it was subject to invasion by indigenous reptiles than marauders from the city. To a hammer, everything looks like a nail. To a computer pioneer, everything looks like technology.

Two years after purchasing a flat-screen, smart TV, I am contemplating a SUHD that accurately shows blacks due to some innovation that only industry geeks understand. Yes, I am tempted to buy a 75 inch curved screen that has roughly four times the definition of a 1080 pixel TV, I now own. But one does not just buy the huge video component one also needs a 7.1 Dolby speaker system to pinpoint the sounds as they appear to emerge from the gigantic screen.

It is new; that is what greatly recommends the upgrade in TV reception, also the size. Bigger is better. But something that big could upset the dogs, who will no doubt bark at the intrusive entertainment, thus preventing my golden ears from detecting the dulcet tones of my 15 speaker sound system. Lets hope that wisdom overcomes the innovative urge, but I do not know at this time which will win out. I am driven to answer the technological urge like any other consumer.

Best judgment should from recent memory tell us that new is not always functional in meeting all the promised hype. When I first got a cell phone, most of the locations I tried to call from or receive calls from were dead areas. If calling from the express ways, then most calls would go through. Many times being one of the first to engage innovation, often does not result in fulfilling the promise as advertised. Sometimes rapid change has glitches that are worked out while you pay for interrupted or less than advertised service. Everyone that had cable television over three decades ago probably has had experience with interrupted service, and many moved on to satellite TV which has its own problems.

Chapter 4

The Genuine Article

How can we know that we are reality centered, that we are genuine, that we have an independent identity to ourselves and not a acculturated average of intermediate dispositions, possessions, cultures and extremes? In order to answer this question we must explore what makes us what we are.

Up until about a century ago most people voluntarily or involuntarily made decisions and judgments by weighing against a tradition, the values and principles which one shared among ones people, a commonality. These were the essential moorings preventing us from being swept away into the vortex of unbridled change. In America this common tide of belief was referred to as a melting pot. Just beyond the middle of the last century we were told by Arthur Schlesinger, Jr. that the melting pot of ideas and beliefs was being lost and the cultural maze of true and self-defining identity was causing our country to lose its ideals and its way. The struggle between cultures, acculturation, was accompanied by the rejection of enculturation of the young leaving them wide open to rebellion having lost their way culturally. Pop culture was then re-identifying to a non-functional, fantastic lifestyle which could changed on a whim, and which had no compulsory history of compliance.

At the same time we were adopting, so called, "tolerance" for others which was not disagreement with the ideas of others, nor punishment differences, but we, in acceptance of their ideas, threw our beliefs into a stagnant pot of ideas no one visited. All except a few belief systems were to be seen tolerantly without drawing distinction or favoritism among tenants and creeds.

We would soon not be able to retrieve our once closely held beliefs. Several decades later we were not only devoid of any creed of conscience but were empty of belief. The core of dedicated belief had been diluted by all other beliefs and our old understandings excoriated. We now had no determinate guidance.

By the middle of the last century a new philosophy arose in Europe. One that would not require an inner belief but would look to the experiential events of life. Existential philosophy, as it was called, tried to impose the weight of experience on an understanding of self. After WW II the existentialist movement gave hope to some that they were finding direction moving through life looking for authentication, that we are defined by our behavior and thoughts and that an essentialism of inner person was narrow and unworkable. Instead of reestablishing our core tenets we looked to experience to ground us without a strong set of beliefs, yet experience has no authoritative context and the effect was to confuse and produce doubt in authenticity as we were being pulled from one experience to the next as if each event had saliency.

Another influence on the modern heart and mind was to come in the form of a philosophy called pragmatism. It had been around for a long time in bits and spurts, but by the beginning of the last century, it began to claim devotees in greater numbers. What ever was immediate and "worked" was taken to stand for the right and true. And proven definitions of true and right were jettisoned for the utility of an action. Furthermore, without actions' certification, nothing in mind was to be held as true or right. All wisdom of the past was lost to the next workable action. Each experience without context was as meaningful as any other.

Although existentialism began on the Continent it spread in its effects to America and dovetailed rather comfortably with pragmatism which accepted the ever changing behavioral definition of persona. This marriage has become well integrated into our national psyche to the extent that pragmatism has become for most Americans, whether declared as such or merely by existential leading, their directing philosophy. The important connection is in the persistent and perennial openness to individual difference. Toleration was generally the only strong "belief" of pragmatism, to provide for self-justification and emotional salubriousness. Since it had no grounding in the inner self, each new idea and experience washed thought and understanding into a larger sea of doubt and confusion. One could never know oneself, since the onslaught of endless experience did not permit context to be established for any duration, no inner direction against new waves of experiential drift and no experience more dependable than the last.

A pragmatic existentialism grew in the lives of average Americans and their leaders. Make no judgments based on tradition, but take what works as the answers to problems from ones singular critique of ones personal and immediate experience.

The genuine article is not what ever works or is viewed through experience immediate and one-off. But without the grounding of enculturation by parents and society and the acculturational friction adjudged against anyones core of values, one may find him- or herself adrift unable to resolve issues and arrive at lasting decisions. We are left to the superficial beliefs that bear no weight of authority and are poisoned by the toxicity of tolerance without tenants.

We are also found to be inauthentic in that our ideas and behaviors are often curtailed by the immediate pressing in of the newest political correctness. Society through media and other associative and acceptable influences, brands our understanding, burns what one should think into the deepest recesses of our superegos and socializations. Our ids and egos are compromised by a given and binding understanding and we weaken the self-defensive nature of our lives to belong and tout the acceptive message.

It is in a conflicting moment of acceptance that the whole of our possibly consistent ideas begin to erode. One by one each of our standards of thought and behavior may be sacrificed to what we are bound in kind to argue. The genuine article of consistent action and instinct may be expunged for the favor of the political correction of our thinking. The instincts, apart from any time or administration, are now no longer able to guide us on our way, but we are watching for the next stimulus-response problem in our path, one that does not seek a logical next problem, but rather where each reaction may stand on its own.

Chapter 5

Temporality

The result of unanalyzed rapid change is that we live our lives in temporal saliency. Each new event or object that enters our lives has no relative merit, all things without essential values to guide us become incorporated without question or ignored while having no reason. Not only is newness not analyzed, as we have seen in the previous chapter, there is no standard remaining to dependably value it. There is no reason to keep or remove newness. It has only newness to recommend itself; when newness is judged no longer on the cutting edge, it can be disposed of for something else or some new experience, any new experience. We are building a society on the cultivation of the new. Innovation is given prominence and preference over everything else without judgment, without care. If innovation is deemed valuable now, that is all that matters. If an object is made obsolete or no longer serves the perfect purpose, if indeed it were to have a purpose, then it can be discarded, thrown on the waste heap of time, and another object will take its place - even smaller with more functions than the last and requiring more time to learn for one cannot be found ignorant of the new.

Technological games wire our reactions to a heightened self-program. There is ultimately little thought but faster responses to what is often the killing of the enemy in game time. If the gamer were to think of the simulation of the program he or she might decide to discontinue playing, but the abstraction of format lets competition flow without the first thought of the realities that are graphically represented. Competition is meant to be quick at speeds not compliant with thought but by raw reflex. The goal is to become so fast and proficient that thought would only slow down the killing. Activity without cognizance induces a rapid, a blind, and numbing commission of thoughtless acts.

Thoughtless acts may reflex the fast pace of life. What do we do quickly? Why do we seem to push on to the next issue or event as if it were the natural thing to do? We speed through meals, time with family giving "quality" not quantity time to our commutes, work and even marriages. We are a culture of illiberal inconstancy.

One example of this that stands out is that many people that vote for candidates make up their minds when they enter the voting booth. Issues and political policies set aside, most are voted for according to the cultural influences in which the person is immersed. If you are a student in a liberal university then you will vote for the most noted of the liberal candidates. If you attend a conservative college, then your choices will probably be limited to conservative politicians. One's dress and personal adornment are more likely to be predictors of voting tendencies than any concern or inclination to candidate policies.

Culture isolates us from our own nascent thoughts and rolls our tendencies into the closest subcultural match. If we look like the cliquish mavens of our surroundings, then we will probably emulate them in choices. Distant influences, if they remain salient over time, may become ones *raison d' être* and subsist even in allegiances long past. On the other hand, rapid change, temporality, may cause the loss of parametric allegiances as well as the innovations of life tweaked for jettisoning old objects and ways. At best, temporality comes to us as waves of change, often sweeping away foundational moorings in their path. An example is the often touted middle-age revolt. A decent and reasonable man buys a red sports car, takes up with the secretary and divorces his wife. Which is the wave in this example is unclear, but all three factors work to bring the man into a crisis, one he does not necessarily understand, that moves fast in bringing down the stability in his life. Desertion of wife and family results in a divided life, one of new-found freedom and the other a remnant of guilt and regret. Values may be thrown on the pyre of passion and destroy the life that has been built with love and care.

We must, at all costs, analyze everything to prevent the parasite of plenty from outgrowing its host. All new must be tested before we buy an electronic device, change our thoughts, change our family, change our friends, change our clothes, which can occupy our time unnecessarily or take away valuable time from our family and friends.

Short lived are the pet rocks and car-grille bras, but value-associated and fixed pillars of our lives, when they are exchanged, never quite make it even back to parity, but, like a parasite, destroy and defame previously held ideas and habits that have served us well. If these ideas and habits displace but have no lingering value, then the short lived life of suspended reason becomes the beginning of mental and value wandering without hope of conceptual mooring or reason to return. One becomes the clothes that he or she wears, the car, the new friends, the new TV or cell phone.

Chapter 6

Subtile Surrender

The most remarkable characteristic of culturation is the stealth with which a vast paradigm change in values can occur possibly without notice. The opportunity for such change is empowered through the way that we see society today: as more and more a social construct in which our friends and enemies are held at an arm length through social networking. A friend may be a person who has shared a selfie or an enemy who has been deleted from a cyber page at some point of interaction or inaction. The friend and enemy may even trade places. Friending and de-friending is an abstraction of contact and through this reversal can come values that are carried over in the switch. One may have hundreds of friends, and one may be only as good a friend as it is possible to keep up with the flow charts of friendships, knowing who knows who, and who has been cut loose from the network. So it is possible with associations that dramatic value changes may occur.

The framework of change allows our acceptance and rejection of innovation and impositions in our "personal life" to evade deep acquisition in real-time and substantial meaning. Social media is designed to take on friendship as a convenience. We only engage a friend when we are in the mood. If we are interested, if not concerned, no matter where we are, we may interrupt any true social commitment by saying, " this is urgent I must take this call." I once had a young person who was discussing house sitting for my wife and I, fumbling with her phone, texting while in conversation with us and apologizing for only giving us interrupted attention. She never interrupted her personal world to engage us fully in ours even as she apologized but never stopped her messaging.

There is focus but not on the presumed object of attention but rather the media that allows the attention. Moving up to the next technological gizmo does not involve the concern about privacy of all concerned, intrusion into what once was considered normal functionality in life or the time taken away from others in person to deal with a cyber world of connectivity. Moving up precludes any discussion about the significance and preemption of a normal life by our habits of toys and a "lite" definition of friendship. In fact the absence of any conversation among family members sitting at a meal but not talking just watching the pictures and icons move on the phone screen comes as close as possible to robotic life, that has ever been imagined before the innovation age. Possibly a better description would be not the age of innovation but the dawn of the dead. In a true sociological understanding these people must be close to the zombie state depicted in movies.

What cannot sneak by these people? What movements and activities are not stumbled through or are not totally overlooked for the feeding on media and "friends." The scenario becomes even more bizarre with techno-geniuses claiming that in the future we will be able to upload our thoughts and personalities and thereby induce immorality — immortality as data in a program and friendship forever through a main frame. The better bet on the future would be that we will all growing texting sized fingers and a ninety degree bend in the cervical section of our necks - adaptations for our electronic social cell phone obligations.

In our rush to be innovative it looks like we could be leaving our humanity behind. I am reminded of the movie from several decades ago called *Blade Runner*, in which robots were concerned that their robotic existence was preordained in time and they were willing to do anything to have a life that mirrored the living, longing for mortality and even possibly immortality. It would seem that the humans were not as dedicated to life as the robots who stood to lose something not quite human life. Life for the living had been taken for granted and the casual ability to recognize the living among the robots had to some extent been lost such that only expert testing could distinguish man from machine.

Ray Kurtzweil, a brilliant inventor and thinker, has proposed that we undertake a robotic existence in having our personalities, memories and thoughts uploaded into a computer where we could live for eternity. Tragedy could be the loss of computer containing our remains much like a sky scrapper repurposing a grave yard.

Our understanding, in light of this challenge to program ourselves, must be a serious indication that we are not grasping our uniqueness and our value as living breathing humans. Uploading ourselves to computers would allow us to shed the mortal coil for an existence without sickness, aging or senility. Kurzweil's goal is immortality, but that term is reserved for living breathing humans not mainframes holding information, which is not heaven. This leaves much to be wished for even in the mind's of social media acolytes. One could still be murdered by taking ones personal program offline or destroying the computer and its hard drive.

We have had the drive and talent to make what ever we wanted, to become what ever we willed. We have slipped and are surrendering to this kind of talk that humanity is way over valued. The spark of man's continuity with the past and the hope of such continued ongoing contact with people of the future is is being devalued. Could a family computer adequately represent the nervous essence of children and grandchildren as we gather around the CPU for a holiday social? We are looking down the barrel of a gun in the hands of a nihilistic monster that would have us put the loss of life and breath in time over the warmth of love and trials of a homeothermic existence. It is strange that the human life that gave us personality and memories that are too valuable to lose will end in the main frame, in human death. We must look forward in the new cyber environment not to new life but physical death, to find the security of our protective circuitry as feeling passes not more slowly through nervous and circulatory retes but through what may be lightening fast hard wiring to speed past any feeling, compassion or empathy. Kurtzweil's new world, if it is allowed to trap us, will see that we do not have measured responses and doubt but the light-speed of assurance of electrons surging through silicon chips.

Chapter 7

Society's Prospects

If our turn from informed consciousness to blind acceptance of ideas and objects comes to fruition, then we may expect a future that controls us or at least we will not be in control of ourselves. This means that our voting, choice of mates, cars, homes, food and church may be determined without our analysis and total understanding. Before you know it, all of these choices will start to push us into a greatly limiting lifestyle such that conflicting ideas will not have much chance to be added to the accumulated choices and resultant values already in place. Engaging ones mind will only lead to frustration and confusion. We must give our thoughts context in order to incorporate them into our lives. When our contextual thoughts are predetermined they will only allow compatible thoughts. Identity will only come from without and successfully challenged beliefs, when values are not analyzed within the context of deeply held and valued positions, will be lost to the new.

We will trade any hope for a true personal essentialism to be lost for the uploading of a collective cultural identity. As we are beginning to see even now there will not be two sides to each argument but a right and a wrong one. Reason to the truth will not be accessed by the mind but only by ones feelings for the composite identity by which we live. These unified feelings will not accept what is foreign to our makeup. Feelings, since we do not have the domain of thought advising us, will never determine whether to go to war or balance the budget because these are understood by rational minds. Fear will become the motivating factor in decisions. Fear of war and never denying oneself money will never see the solution to problems that face our culture. Laws will continue to topple at the hands of special interest groups and fear of confrontation will ease the way. Those not spared will be the fearful who cave in the wake of oppressors who eschew fear and self-control.

A loss of our civilization to the emotivists will only be surpassed in effect by the fall of our country and civilization to the militant hoards that will once again attempt to rule the world at the expense of this country. What America has been fighting, master/slave roles, can be reinstated by the unbridled competition for things and position driven by feelings, felt needs. The culture may see the class system return in the form of individualistic terrorism where everyone is seen as subservient to the individual who through opposition is affected through an aggressive self-supporting initiative.

We tend to follow the strongest if not totalitarian leaders. We have opted for play and indoctrination when children are put through T-ball and Little League sports. If it were only the socialization of children that were involved then there would be no reason to warn against child athletics, but the idea is most often thoughtless: creativity of activity is being stifled by the organized sports for those three year olds to those in their seventies. Before such sports authorities arose all children seemed to be able to organize their own sports: football, soccer, basketball and tennis not to mention maul ball and cork ball which must have arisen from creativity restricted to the limitations of space and materials. The rules in sports are supposed to show children that they cannot have their way and that adult supervision offers the better settling of game disputes, but being able to play together, just children, requires that the young learn how to govern themselves and respect a fixed set of rules, something lost today on adults as well. I do remember getting mad and going home in the middle of a game, but I always came back and we worked out the problems among the neighborhood children without parents intervention. Today's children unless they have a realistic expectation of a college or professional sports career, working out the techniques of the sport is not as valuable as the social creativity of getting along with others without adult supervision. Possibly an adult could have grown more in character by self-regulation than by being told what to do or even playing a game for which many of the the children have little interest for what they can both learn about the game and the way to get along with their peers, especially when being forced into play by a controlling parent.

Sports in youth offers the pattern for educational and work careers. Fit the mold; do not branch out on your own. Some of the most successful young people in our country have had little other-directed formal education, like Steve Jobs and Bill Gates, but have creatively found an indelible place in our society. That is not to say that education is bad, all evidence would indicate that college degrees and graduate degrees will, on average, be a boon to the pocketbooks of those well educated students. People with advanced degrees can change the world. Students, what ever their area of study, will create nothing meaningful, if they do not continue to learn post-college and become life-long self-learners. Often the restrictions placed on them are the result of the area of educational concentration — creative life is constrained when areas of study and expertise narrow the scope or inquiry. In most college classrooms today questioning and inquiry are not sanctioned particularly, if inquiry calls into question professorial reason. This type of learning can curtail creative learning and lead us as a country into passive acceptance of directions and the willing to not question but to say yes..

Creativity is largely missing today; for some because they think outside the box and move ahead of those less motivated to learn. One of our most important products has been the creative genius of our people. Today many young graduates are looking at a narrowing list of jobs available or, for their studies, few to no jobs at all. The larger point is that being constrained from childhood, to be a team player, does not always allow the creative growth to take place that would allow making the most of ones educational qualifications. Creativity is being trained out of our children. It was amazing to see in the secondary education classroom how few students are capable of independent thought. Most of the children I taught over my twenty year tenure in secondary education had little working creativity. Most would have me tell them what they needed to know for the test. Few had the ability or the inclination to develop their own deeper formal understanding and inquiry into the curriculum material.

Chapter 8

Secure and Cold

The advantage that cultured bacteria have over humans is that many bacteria can remain dormant over time until an appropriate environment, water and food are provided. For modern humans the flow of life with change is often blindingly rapid and there is not the pressing need to be who we really are, growing into authentic organisms of the species. Moderns are anything but dormant and change often persists resulting in inauthenticity, while bacteria can be only what they are — clones within the colony. To belong, to be current in all ways has left us wanting to always be in the center of life. Humans, overpowered by the temporality that persists in replacing the old, through indiscriminate change and without analysis, but accepting all, has left the nouveau longing for security not appropriated with such change. As a country we accelerate our need by adopting the new as if the innovation will show the way and give us the key to the vacuum deep in our hearts. The key to our existence is not found in innovation, yet we await its next rollout. No time for the one thing that we need, protection of who we are out of time if necessary. But our drive is to the new, counting on rapid replacement to garner the security that we want, a perpetual place, a magniloquent recommendation of values that are unchanging.

Some have come to believe that merely being taken care of will give the freedom to become something that will define and secure. Almost half of Americans now get some assistance from the government. Many want to be taken care of, to become what ever the culture requires, to keep us funded and safe. Millennials, also referred to as Generation Y, are seen by many as monolithic, lacking the determination to take risks with many lacking the entrepreneurial spirit of past generations. Having a singular social orientation such that the ultimate realities of maintaining a system of entitlements are not considered: they do not dwell on the tremendous debt which they will inherit and the degraded lifestyle to which they will necessarily succumb. The future is cold as it now stands before us without a realistic strategy for surviving our willingness to take all we can take from a broken and unpromising economic and social system. Our countries financial security may already be lost.

When we adopt a lifestyle and view of culture without analyzing what we do and why, we may gain a false security. Our pragmatism takes up the last line of defending our security by saying: it must be right and right for us, if it works for us. If alchemy and witchcraft could solve our problems, it would still be preferable to look to science and reason which could offer solutions to our problems. The difference is that analysis is required to reasonable understanding. Without understanding our lot is chaotic behavior, inconsistent thought and living other than a reasoned life: like bacteria in the throes of the media.

Conclusion

Can we claim anything that we do or say or own is the result of our choice? The culture in which we live may control, if not all, then many of our activities, objects and even thoughts that influence who we are. There may be little choice. Many of us are being forced into a common mould. Those that give us jobs and friends and relatives from whom we derive self-expression may be channeling us into a smaller world. These and other forces may expect us to seamlessly merge with a sanctioned world view. The only choices that we can make on our own are the choice of conditioned sub-groups and subcultures with whom we choose to associate ourselves. But even then, smaller choices made for us point us toward our rigid group associations and the concomitant scaffolding, the directing structure that inheres in those groups. If you wear black clothing, black finger nail polish and dye your hair black you will not be asked to associate with the hoi polloi. Average persons do not present themselves as Gothics, who live in bleak quarters and seek out graves on the weekends with friends. No, we gravitate to those who best represent our habits and habitats. We can dress for Wall Street, for a failed lifestyle, or any lifestyle in between.

It is interesting that we are not talking about only two extremes for association, but each of us is an average of some extreme representations of accepted and unaccepted standards. We may want to look like a vampire or one of its victims, but we will only approach the standard asymtotically. We will probably never look like the undead or, on the other end of the spectrum, an oligarch in a ten thousand dollar suit, but may merely fall in with the best available approximation of our pre-directed culturation.

The things that we buy tell our story of association all too well. I may buy a Lexus claiming it is the best car on the road, but at some level I am identifying with an affluent upper culture. Where I shop and my address may not allow me to find acceptance with the rich, but I can have a bit of passing recognition for my station in life, or at least my pseudo-association by the recognition of rich passing motorists.

Several hundred years ago, when those in the European courts of rule dressed extravagantly, posing ruin to the financial stability of the realm, only the royal few could afford the latest fashion. Indeed these royals created the fashion of the rich. No peon could dress and live in the manner of the kings and queens. Today their is available to many the dress of the rich and famous. We all can dress like the stars: blue jeans, washed out denim shirts and scuffed-up shoes. We are being groomed in the entertainment motif, and we may even adopt the same green lifestyle and the same liberal political leanings. Our lives may not require that we study and understand positions we merely change our beliefs like the chameleon blanching its color on a protective background.We may find what we believe to be security here. And yet change is unavoidable. Poised to change, as the background changes, is the easiest way to be accepted: but a changing environment brings changes to its inhabitants, sending us on another guest for identity and authenticity.

The cultivation discussed here is not the enculturation by parents of children in their care nor the struggle between opposing world views. The culturation in discussion is that of blanket acceptance of ones unplanned but recognizable lifestyle and even the ideas that are assimilated in bulk and through which the individual has not thought.

The story was told that in the early years of the last century that socialites would give parties and hob nob with the Russian Bolsheviks in order to appear involved in the plight of the poor and uncared for. This was not the result of a deep social concern or study, but a distance threat to that which others did have concern, if not revolutionary agendas to displace the rich and raise up the workers, who were felt to be deserving of a social upheaval at the expense of the rich. Mrs. Astor would not have had a wish to have her position challenged, but it was a bit of a Tom Wolf excursion into the dodgier side of revolutionary life without really getting dirty nor it costing anything valuable.

Socialites and celebrities do not have to live with radicals. They are not personally held by the necessary values but by adventure which they can exit anytime. Living with radical ideas or impersonal philosophies one does not have to come to the front for acceptance or stand in authority in completeness, for, if one does adopt changing factors one may never see formal acceptance only the surrender tokens that mark them, that may ultimately change their arguments. When confronted on core issues despite being radical to general beliefs one may accept without substantial supporting evidence and argument a partial position until, with time and circumstance, that acquiescence may force the complete assimilation of a new lifestyle and a comfortable subset. This is a change from the outside rather than from reason and restraint. We take the outer position for protection only to find that the argument begins its travel inward, possibly changing our look and ultimately establishing a new interiority.

Authenticity was lost in the sixties. People were changed from the outside in by ideas that were not so much processed as worn by feeling. One cannot authenticate oneself alone; it is up to others to do that with us. There are many who do not look for authentication, but, those that do not strive for a genuine identity in today's environment of borrowed individuality risk may become clones. Under the pressure imposed by the sixties revolutionaries and the morally bankrupt, the culture of ease and rebellion changed the direction of action possibly for all time. The rebellion against parental authority and even the government was complete from the home to the ultimate authority of the law. The children of those rebel are now often the grand parents of families that have failed to bring their offspring to a truly comfortable and secure maturity. Flexible goals and self-taught morality have left these children and grandchildren in an emotional identity flux.

The existential goal of obtaining through experience, and not through blind suggestion, supports authenticity which is impossible without dedicated purpose and emotional stability among life experiences that are analyzed and thus controlled by an inner foundational essentialism. In today's indecisiveness, unable to hold to a personal position of trust and belief, the individual is unable to become stable in maturity of direction and persona. No one is truly genuine; no one is original in life's choices in the sense that those events that drive us to make decisions have been avoided as we question what we should take from experience and what we should save. There is little to no direction determined to be preferable to other directions from other events and experiences if each event is not analyzed. We may shuffle, emotively coast through experiences finding only those influences to which we are drawn. When there is no established beliefs that guide and direct our actions and attitudes, we in effect, take unreasoned positions and may even fail to take sides. We are inauthentic because we are unable to reach a place of distinction for our lives. We are guided by flirtations with novelty rather than by the values which guide and direct to give consistency and authenticity to our thoughts, attitudes and behaviors. The Culture amid all of its many cultures, redirects or better disorients us as we weave our way though distractions, obstructions and hard decisions. Our disposition is to take the easy way not necessarily the more authentic way to what we hope will be happiness and integrity.

The reason we bend to cultural influences has to do with the seductive nature of change. Culture is a confabulation of many conversations by unweighted averaging of many dispositions and non-contentments. Culture is behavior, products of both attitudes and objects and the progress of intimations which find modifiable persistence and alteration. We listen for and embrace new expressions by association with the deliverer, we become one with the fashion of belief.

There is the confabulated culture, yes, but the unspoken culture which defines as well. The term pigs, which came to be synonymous with the police in the sixties, spread across the country from San Francisco to New York spoken by every hippie and every buttoned-down-shirt would-be-hippie. Likewise, "blow my mind," "far out," "freaked out" and many more terms of the drug subculture came into common usage and many remain today as part of the commonly spoken argot of teens and young adults. These terms are used by non-drug users even today as if they were derivative of high culture.

The exercise of pressure politics moves terms ahead in our usage and the ideas they represent. Choice seems to be a term that has come to represent for most people a term of ones right. Even many of the Pro-lifers use the term choice, which if they were to examine this term it would be found to do nothing for their cause but to conform the argument into freedoms and liberties. When the opposition to abortion takes the term choice out of a debate about morality and places it into the political ring; right-to-life suffers. Compromised terms and thoughts exact unclarified wills on the culture and it is altered, shifting every so slightly or in great leaps to modify cultural values.

Without a national discussion the legislation to legalize same-sex marriage has moved behind its rapid public acceptance. For many the "right" of men or women as citizens to marry seems oppressive since heterosexual couples have no restrictions placed on them, but the fallout from such actions changes everything. But must we accept a legal position?

Why not triadic, polygamous or bestial marriages? The government does have a horse in this race. It is called procreation and determines our ability to stand as a viable country by fecund measure for a sustainable population. The problem is that broadening the traditional definition of marriage can and does redefine its meaning in terms of procreative potential. Since same-sex marriage or co-habitation has become more widely accepted, the adoption of children and death and health benefits may offer challenges to the capitalistic system. Adoption by same-sex couples was given legitimacy automatically, as well as family life and death benefits extended by employers to mirror those of heterosexual couples with their own children who have flesh in the game. Benefits without responsibility? Any homosexual couple who wishes to have children must see themselves as derivative and doing nothing to supply a strong number of citizens in each generation. All of these considerations piggybacking on the legality of marriage, have for most passed under the political radar, for to question heterosexual marriage is not politically correct or potentially legal. When acceptance is given without deeper consideration we have moved farther but without thought of accompanying fallout that might be a third rail to our progress.

People exact their wills on the culture and it is altered, shifted every so slightly or in great leaps to then modify culture. As people come and go, the culture is changed. People are invited while others are denied entry into the practice of culture or into communities. Where one may deny a culture-novelty flaw others may allow entry so it may find its way into the core of group identity and possibly find a place. Culturation often slips in where reason has failed to vet or discourage. Culturation moves away from that standard of thought and behavior and holds a line that challenges the established culture, without a platform for reasonable manipulation: manipulation and change is almost always to be seen to come to fruition in time.

The affirmation of those allowed to enter core groups with dedicated purpose, produces an altered direction and value in both. Those that move away from that standard of thought and behavior tend to hold a line that challenges the culture, but, without a platform for opposition, effects are isolated, vilified and prevented from being absorbed into the leadership message of the larger group, and may even find its way back to enculturated values of childhood.

How do we work to avoid mindless culturation? Several strategies may help minimize it effects and increase chances of finding authenticity. First, try and reason through ones support of any consideration. Not because the people around you believe one side to be correct, rather because you have looked at both sides or multiple sides and you have reasoned clearly to a logical defense. Your solid premise should not be that it merely serves yourself.

Second, surround yourself with people who take all sides of the argument. Don't gravitate to a belief system because the people you hang out with are cool. Being cool is not a pre-requisite for holding a beliefa and does not provide context. By selecting a position without reason, there may be perimetric considerations that are assumed through this error, while other beliefs or ideas that are subsumed from ones essentialistic foundation is held to be unworthy.

Next do not chose friends by their clothes. In the sixties many young people were drawn into the hippie culture, at least superficially, by affecting the hippie look and drawl. Don't be trapped by lazily adopting some look, car preference or locus for living. Challenge your own reason for a precluding precedence. Break the bonds of assumption: think all things through. Do not let assumptions of recency grow understandings concentrically about your ill-gotten position like a pearl from continued irritation grows the deposition of hard nacre. This process can begin with the affectation of fashion.

All thoughts, actions and objects must be tested for any effect on authenticity. Even though authenticity is not the product of individual effects alone, we are in a constant state of flux for our doing and thinking and for those effects from our environment. The totality of effects is often by an unweighted averaging of many ideas, by the progress of intimations which find modifiable persistence and eventually alteration. There is confabulated culture and the unspoken culture which also defines us. Not all effects will lead to culturation, but question all change. Be on guard and look for alterations in your environment.

Above all, our God given humanity must tower over any understanding, not by politicians or seers. We must be dedicated to the knowledge that if it cannot be reasoned humanely then it should not be known by reason. The enslavement of moderns to fads and objects of short lived value is degradation of lives, hour by hour and day by day. Those that would make us be willing to sacrifice our bodies for the stars and times, pushing us to enter into a devil's bargain of cold security, should be seen for whom they are. Those that would perpetually contemporize us, denying our shorter future in flesh and caring must not be given the power to prevent our quest to find our identity and authentication. Time is the river that can flow through a world of uncharted experience for good, to bad ends, but truly and personally, but it must be scrutinized for defections.